⊕ WORLD BOOK'S
CELEBRATIONS AND RITUALS AROUND THE WORLD

World Book, Inc.
a Scott Fetzer Company
Chicago

This edition published in the United States of America by World Book, Inc., Chicago. WORLD BOOK and the GLOBE DEVICE are registered trademarks or trademarks of World Book, Inc.

World Book, Inc.
233 North Michigan Avenue
Chicago, IL 60601 U.S.A.

For information about other World Book publications, visit our Web site http://www.worldbook.com, or call 1-800-WORLDBK (967-5325).
For information about sales to schools and libraries, call:
1-800-975-3250 (United States); 1-800-837-5365 (Canada).

In the same series:
Harvest Celebrations
Birth and Growing Up Celebrations
National Celebrations
Spring Celebrations

Copyright © 2003, McRae Books Srl

Via dei Rustici, 5—Florence, Italy.
info@mcraebooks.com

Library of Congress Cataloging-in-Publication Data
New year celebrations.
    p. cm. —(World Book's celebrations and rituals around the world)
    Includes index.
    Summary: Describes how the coming of the new year is celebrated in different countries and by different cultures around the world.
    ISBN: 0-7166-5006-1
    1. New Year—Cross-cultural studies—Juvenile literature. [1. New Year. 2. Festivals.] I. World Book, Inc. II Series.
GT4905 .N39 2002
394.2614--dc21   2002027041

Printed and bound in Hong Kong by C&C Offset

1 2 3 4 5 6 7 8 9 10 09 08 07 06 05 04 03 02

McRae Books:
Publishers: Anne McRae and Marco Nardi
Series Editor: Loredana Agosta
Graphic Design: Marco Nardi
Layout: Sebastiano Ranchetti
Picture Research: Laura Ottina, Loredana Agosta
Cutouts: Filippo delle Monache, Alman Graphic Design
Text: Matilde Bardi pp. 6, 10–13, 36–39, 42–43; Catherine Chambers pp. 40–41; Anita Ganeri pp. 20–25; Cath Senker pp. 30–31; Paige Weber pp. 8–9, 14–19, 26–29, 32–35

Illustrations: Inklink Firenze, Studio Stalio (Alessandro Cantucci, Fabiano Fabbrucci, Andrea Morandi, Ivan Stalio), Paola Ravaglia, Paula Holguin, Lorenzo Cecchi

Color Separations: Litocolor, Florence (Italy)

World Book:
Editorial: Maureen Liebenson, Sharon Nowakowski
Research: Paul Kobasa, Cheryl Graham, Thomas Ryan Sullivan
Text Processing: Curley Hunter, Gwendolyn Johnson
Proofreading: Anne Dillon

Acknowledgements
The Publishers would like to thank the following photographers and picture libraries for the photos used in this book.
t=top; tl=top left; tc=top center; tr=top right; c=center; cl=center left; cr=center right; b= bottom; bl=bottom left; bc=bottom center; br=bottom right
A.S.A.P Picture Library: 28c, 28b, 29cl, 29br; Corbis/ De Bellis 21tr; Corbis/ Grazia Neri 25; Dinodia 21cl, 23bl; Farabola Foto: 10t, 12b; Lonely Planet Images: Greg Elms 20t, 23br; Kraig Lieb 25tr; Francis Linzee Gordan 40cr; Adriadne Van Zandberaen 41tr; Ross Barnett 42cl; Peter Hines 42cr; Marco Lanza: 25b, 37tr; Marco Nardi/McRae Books Archives: 12cl, 12tr; The Image Works: 6cl, 6cr, 14tl,15c, 15bl, 16t, 17tr, 18b, 19t, 23t, 24c, 31c, 31b, 32b, 34c, 35tr, 35c, 36c, 37tl, 37cr, 38c, 41b, 43tr; Worldbridges Tibet 24b (http://worldbridges.com/tibet/links.html)

WORLD BOOK'S

CELEBRATIONS AND RITUALS AROUND THE WORLD

NEW YEAR'S
CELEBRATIONS

Table of Contents

New Year's Celebrations

Introduction

New Year's Day is one of the oldest and most widely celebrated holidays in the world. New Year's celebrations are both serious and festive. In many cultures, the New Year's holiday is a time for people to reflect on their actions over the past year and resolve to live a better life. It is also a time to celebrate with parades, parties, fireworks, and good food.

For many ancient people, the new year began at harvesttime. For example, the Yam Festival now celebrated throughout much of West Africa marks both the harvest of this important vegetable crop and the start of the new year. For other people, New Year's Day was tied to the renewal of nature that accompanied the arrival of spring. In some countries, such as China and Korea, the start of the new year is still celebrated in spring and is known both as New Year and Spring Festival. Among other cultures, New Year's Day celebrates folk traditions or an important religious person or event. In some cases, folk traditions and religion have mingled, such as in Bulgaria, where St. Basil's Day celebrations have clear pagan (pre-Christian) roots. Whenever New Year's Day is celebrated and whatever its origins, it is almost always a time of joy when families and friends meet, eat, and have fun.

These Tibetan monks are blowing ceremonial horns. During Losar, the Tibetan New Year, monasteries are at the center of the celebration.

Wearing new clothes is a common way to celebrate the new year. A change of wardrobe symbolizes new beginnings, and clean, fresh clothing puts everyone in the party mood!

Not everyone celebrates the new year on January 1. Although this is the most commonly celebrated day, many other dates throughout the year mark, or have marked, the beginning of the yearly calendar. This chart lists just a sample of New Year's Days from around the world.

Julius Caesar, top left, created a new calendar in 46 B.C. with January 1 as the start of the new year. Before then, the ancient Romans celebrated New Year's Day on March 25.

NEW YEAR'S DAY ALSO HAS ITS SOLEMN OR SERIOUS SIDE. For Jewish people, for example, it is a time of self-examination, when people search their hearts for wrongs they may have done in the previous year, and vow to do better in the coming year.

NEW YEAR'S DAYS

JANUARY
1
The world's most celebrated holiday

14
Eastern Orthodox Calendar New Year

MARCH
21
Baha'i New Year

21
Zoroastrian New Year's Day

APRIL
13 or 14
Sikh New Year's Day

13 or 14
Solar New Year, celebrated in Southeast Asia under many names

JUNE
21
New Year's Day for the Aymara people in Bolivia

SEPTEMBER
11 or 12
Coptic New Year

New Year's Day in the Past

This large Calendar Stone, which is about 12 feet in diameter, was created by the Aztecs. The Aztecs ruled part of what now is known as Mexico until the 1500's. They believed in cycles of destruction, followed by rebirth.

As early as 3500 B.C., people planned their New Year's celebrations around the most important dates in their calendars. The earliest recorded New Year's ritual occurred in Mesopotamia, where the Sumerians celebrated the renewal of their land's fertility. The ancient Egyptians marked the annual flooding of the Nile River with grand processions. The Celts celebrated New Year's Day at the start of winter with bonfires, feasts, dancing, and revelry. Many modern New Year's customs derive from ancient times.

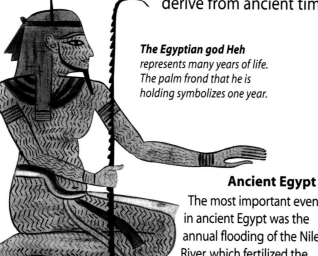

The Egyptian god Heh represents many years of life. The palm frond that he is holding symbolizes one year.

Ancient Egypt

The most important event in ancient Egypt was the annual flooding of the Nile River, which fertilized the land. The floods arrived soon after Sothis (Sirius), the brightest star in the night sky, appeared just before sunrise. This marked the start of the new year. The Egyptians celebrated with religious processions and feasting.

The Sumerian New Year

The earliest known New Year's celebrations took place in ancient Sumer, the first great civilization in Mesopotamia. The king temporarily gave up his crown and prayed for his subjects' forgiveness. A priest then restored the king's title. Next, the king paraded to a sanctuary and acted out the fertility drama of the Sacred Marriage between Ishtar, the goddess of love, and her husband, the shepherd Tammuz, *above*. All subsequent Mesopotamian civilizations enacted similar rituals.

BEFORE JULIUS CAESAR REFORMED THE ROMAN CALENDAR, the ancient Romans celebrated New Year's Day on March 25.

IN ANCIENT GREECE, New Year's celebrations coincided with spring and the Feast of Dionysus (the god of wine). A baby, representing rebirth, was placed in a basket and paraded through the city streets.

The Roman god Janus had two faces, as shown on this coin. He could look backward and forward at the same time.

Ancient Rome

Janus was the ancient Roman god of entrances and exits and the guardian of new ventures. The Romans believed that at midnight on New Year's Eve, Janus looked over the past year and blessed the new one. Our word *January* comes from his name.

CALENDARS

A calendar is a system used to fix the beginnings, ends, and other parts of the year. Most ancient civilizations used lunar calendars based on the moon's phases. They gradually discovered, however, that the lunar year did not correspond to Earth's orbit of the sun, which takes 365.2422 days. They needed a solar calendar. The ancient Egyptians fixed the year at 365 days. Julius Caesar applied Egyptian ideas to the lunar Roman calendar in 46 B.C. He added a leap year and fixed January 1 as New Year's Day. In 1582, Pope Gregory XIII changed the Julian calendar and established the Gregorian calendar many countries use today.

Celtic calendar

Christian calendar

THE ENGLISH WORD *CALENDAR* derives from *kalendae*, the Latin word for the first day of the month.

The early Christian calendar, left, *shows the system devised by Julius Caesar.*

The Celts

The ancient Celtic year began on November 1. It was celebrated during the festival of Samhain (Summer's End). October 31, New Year's Eve, was a wild time when the barriers between the worlds of the living and the dead were believed to disappear. The Celts built bonfires to ward off evil spirits and danced and feasted. Halloween has evolved from Samhain.

Ancient Persia

Darius I (550? – 486 B.C.) ruled the Persian Empire at the height of its power, when it controlled lands from modern-day Libya to Pakistan. During Nawruz, the celebration of the spring equinox, delegates from across the empire traveled to Persepolis, the capital, to present tributes to the emperor.

The Celtic calendar, far left, *was found in France and dates to around 10 B.C. It shows the month of Samon, which ran from mid-October to mid-November and marked the end of summer and the beginning of the Celtic new year.*

This illustration shows the magnificent procession to *Darius the Great's palace at Persepolis during the ancient Persian New Year's festival of Nawruz.*

The Lion Dance is performed by two people in a lion costume. They are accompanied by musicians playing drums, gongs, and cymbals. A visit from the dancers in the first few days of the new year is considered a sign of good luck.

The Far East

A magnificent display of fireworks explodes over Hong Kong harbor to celebrate the new year. The ancient Chinese invented gunpowder in about 850 B.C. The use of fireworks dates to about the same time.

THE FAR EAST

The Far East is the easternmost part of Asia. Asia extends from Africa and Europe in the west to the Pacific Ocean in the east. The northernmost part of the continent is in the Arctic. In the south, Asia ends in the tropics near the equator. Traditionally, the term Far East has referred to China, Japan, North Korea, South Korea, Taiwan, and eastern Siberia in Russia. Southeast Asia includes Borneo, Brunei, Cambodia, East Timor, Indonesia, Laos, Malaysia, Myanmar, the Philippines, Singapore, Thailand, and Vietnam.

Celebrating in China

Spring Festival or Chinese New Year is the oldest and most important festival in China and in Chinese communities around the world. This lunar holiday is celebrated on the second new moon after the winter solstice. This means that the date changes every year, falling somewhere between January 20 and February 21. Traditionally, the festival lasts for 15 days, although modern celebrations usually last only 2 or 3 days. Chinese New Year is seen as a time of renewal. Preparations for the New Year's festival begin several days beforehand. People thoroughly clean their houses from top to bottom. They do not clean on New Year's Day for fear that good fortune will be swept away. People also repay their debts, buy new clothes and shoes to wear on the first day of the new year, and have their hair cut. As the old year draws to a close, people think about their mistakes and failures. They decide how to act better in the new year and what they can do to bring good luck to themselves and their families.

The Chinese sign for spring appears often during New Year's celebrations.

THE STORY OF THE NIAN MONSTER

Many years ago, a wild beast appeared in a country village and destroyed the crops and the village itself. The next year it returned and the same thing happened. The following year, the villagers were ready for it. They set off firecrackers, lit all their lamps, and decorated their houses in red. They made loud music and danced until they scared away the beast.

IT IS CONSIDERED LUCKY TO WEAR ALL NEW CLOTHING and shoes on New Year's Day. Stepping outside on New Year's morning in old clothing and shoes, on the other hand, is believed to bring bad luck in the coming year.

The Dragon Dance

Dragons are an important part of many Chinese festivals, including New Year's. Each year, troupes of young Chinese men and women with drums and cymbals perform the noisy and colorful dragon dance in memory of the beast who once terrorized the country village. The dance is believed to chase away bad luck in the coming year.

The Festival Begins

Chinese New Year is a time when families and friends come together to eat special meals and to exchange gifts. There are parties at home and parades and processions in the streets. New Year's Eve and New Year's Day are celebrated as family feast days. On New Year's Eve, all members of the family (many of whom travel long distances to attend) are reunited around a banqueting table, and a communal feast known as weilu (surrounding the stove) is held. Traditional ceremonies begin with family members sealing the cracks around the door and windows with red paper to prevent evil from entering. The male head of the family then leads the family in making offerings to household gods and to the family ancestors. The whole family stays awake all night, eating, drinking wine, singing, and telling stories. As dawn breaks, they unseal the main door, throwing it open to allow favorable influences to rush in. This is accompanied by the explosion of long whips of firecrackers.

Spirit guards such as this one are hung on doorways for Chinese New Year to protect the family against evil and to usher in prosperity.

At a temple in Singapore, left, red lanterns symbolize the Lantern Festival, which is held on the 15th, and last, day of Chinese New Year. Chinese traditionally make pilgrimages to temples in the days after Chinese New Year.

ORANGES AND TANGERINES ARE TRADITIONAL GIFTS for friends and family at New Year's festivities. They are also a favorite temple and cemetery offering to ancestors during the two-week long celebration. Tangerines with their leaves still attached ensure that family ties remain secure.

ANCESTOR WORSHIP

Respect for parents and elders is very important in Chinese families. This respect continues even after death. Ancestors are remembered and honored throughout New Year's celebrations. Offerings are made at family meals as well as at local temples, where photos and ancestor tablets are placed in their honor. Incense is burned both in the home and at the temple. Incense is a mixture of sweet-smelling gums and balsams. It is usually made in powder form or in sticks and burns with a delicate fragrance.

New Year's cards with the traditional greeting "Kung-hsi fa-ts'ai" or "Gong Xi Fa Cai" ("Wishing you success and prosperity!") are exchanged among family members and friends.

New Year's Eve is the busiest day of the year for most stores and markets. People buy food, gifts, and drinks for family and friends. This store is selling specially prepared baskets of fruit and sweets.

THE FOOD

Vast amounts of food are prepared during Chinese New Year. Special dishes are chosen to bring good luck in the coming year. A chicken is served to ensure prosperity. A circular or octagonal candy tray called the Tray of Togetherness offers a selection of sweets, each one symbolizing happiness, long life, good health, or other good wishes.

In wealthy households, the Kitchen God may be represented by a handsome statue like the one shown here. In other homes, a printed icon or tablet, like the red tablet shown here, serves in its place. Traditionally, honey is applied to the god's mouth before he makes his report—either to stick his lips together or to make him speak sweetly!

New Year's Day

The day begins early with children greeting their parents and receiving Hong Bao (Red Packets) with money. Married couples give these envelopes to children and young adults. This gift is considered lucky for both the receiver and the giver. For several days, the family goes door-to-door to offer greetings to relatives, friends, and neighbors. During this time, old grudges are forgiven. Hosts provide delicious foods for their guests, who bring gifts and warm greetings.

The Kitchen God

The God of the Hearth or Cooking Stove (known as the Kitchen God) is the most common household deity. He is placed in the kitchen (the traditional hub of the house), from where he observes the behavior of each family member all year. On the 24th day of the lunar month before New Year's Day, he goes up to heaven to report on how the family has behaved.

ACCORDING TO ONE SUPERSTITION, THE FIRST PERSON YOU MEET on New Year's morning can influence your fortune for the rest of the year.

THE CHINESE HOROSCOPE

Unlike the horoscope used in the West, which is based on the months of the year, the Chinese horoscope is based on a system of 12 years, each of which is named after an animal.

The Pig
1959, 1971, 1983, 1995, 2007. You are honest and reliable. You have many friends.

The Rat
1948, 1960, 1972, 1984, 1996, 2008. You are kind and cheerful.

The Dog
1958, 1970, 1982, 1994, 2006. You are honest and loyal. You make a very good friend.

The Ox
1949, 1961, 1973, 1985, 1997, 2009. You are strong and faithful (and sometimes stubborn too).

The Rooster
1957, 1969, 1981, 1993, 2005. You are a little proud. You are good at talking and writing.

The Tiger
1950, 1962, 1974, 1986, 1998, 2010. You are powerful and brave. You are a good leader.

The Monkey
1956, 1968, 1980, 1992, 2004. You are clever and agile. You can also be selfish at times.

The Rabbit
1951, 1963, 1975, 1987, 1999, 2011. You are happy, successful, and lucky.

The Sheep
1955, 1967, 1979, 1991, 2003, 2015. You are calm, gentle, and kind, although you worry too much.

The Dragon
1952, 1964, 1976, 1988, 2000, 2012. You enjoy good health and are always full of energy.

The Horse
1954, 1966, 1978, 1990, 2002, 2014. You are kind, cheerful, work hard, and expect a lot from others.

The Snake
1953, 1965, 1977, 1989, 2001, 2013. You are wise, strong, and always think carefully before acting.

A girl and two small boys play together at a New Year's celebration in one of a series of famous paintings created during the Qing Dynasty (1644-1911). The child in the center is holding a bunch of lucky lotus blossoms.

Every traditional Chinese home has blooming plants and flowers at New Year's celebrations to symbolize rebirth and new growth. It is considered especially lucky if a household plant blooms on New Year's Day, for this foretells a year of prosperity. Plum blossom, bamboo, pine sprigs, pussy willow, and water lilies are the most common New Year's plants.

Oshogatsu in Japan

On New Year's Eve, each Japanese family places a decoration called a kadomatsu at the front entrance to their house. In Japanese, kado means house entrance, and matsu means pine tree. A kadomatsu is made of pine branches and can include bamboo and plum tree twigs. It symbolizes longevity and good luck for the household. Japanese people display the kadomatsu for two weeks, a period known as matsunouchi (inside the pine).

OMENS AND
TRADITIONS

When going to sleep on New Year's Day, a Japanese person hopes to dream of Mount Fuji, a hawk, or an eggplant—all favorable omens for the coming year.

The words for Happy New Year! are, Akemashite, Omedeto Gozaimasu!

According to an old Japanese custom, a person is 1 year old at birth and 2 years old on the next New Year's Day. Until the 1800's, all birthdays were celebrated on January 1.

This jubako is packed with traditional Japanese New Year's foods called osechi-ryori. Each dish or ingredient has a special meaning.

Traditional Foods

Throughout the three-day festival of Sanganichi, everyone eats special, traditional foods called osechi-ryori. Osechi-ryori is prepared beforehand so that no one needs to cook during the holiday. Families leave some osechi-ryori on a small table as an offering to the household gods. They pack the rest into colorful, lacquered boxes of several layers called jubako. Each ingredient and dish in osechi-ryori has a symbolic meaning. Datemaki (a rolled omelet) symbolizes progress in learning. Kazunoko (prepared herring roe) symbolizes a wish for many children. A white radish symbolizes long life. Mochi (a rice cake) promotes good fortune and perfect harmony.

Japanese people believe that each new year is separate from other years. So as the old year ends, they perform a ritual called Toshikoshi: They settle their debts and clean their homes to prepare for life anew. Oshogatsu, the New Year's festival, begins on January 1 with a three-day holiday called Sanganichi. Before Japan adopted the Gregorian Calendar in 1873, the lunar calendar determined when the new year began. Oshogatsu is an auspicious time, when people visit shrines, draw fortunes, and study dreams for omens of the coming year. It is also a joyous occasion, as people read beautiful New Year's cards and eat special, symbolic foods. Children receive gifts of money in envelopes called otoshidama. Most people rest during the holiday, but a few stores stay open so that children can spend their money.

The traditional method of pounding steamed rice to create mochi, called mochitsuki, is a very popular, fun activity during the festival celebrations. These people are performing mochitsuki-odori, which is a special dance done during the rice-pounding ceremony.

On Ganjitsu, the first day of the new year, postal workers deliver bundles of New Year's postcards, called nengajo, from friends and colleagues. The card below shows daruma dolls, whose eyes represent fulfilled wishes (painted) or desires (unpainted). People buy new daruma dolls for the new year.

Visiting the Shrine

According to tradition, the first day of the year predicts one's fate for the new year. Therefore, January 1 should be filled with joy and relaxation. That morning, people visit Shinto shrines to secure good fortune. They make offerings, clap their hands to summon the gods, and pray. Outside, they buy omikuji— fortunes written on white paper strips—and tie them to trees. Omikuji represent hopes for the new year. People also place paper strips called fuda, which ward off evil, inside miniature household shrines.

These white paper amulets, called omikuji, have been tied to a branch and left at a shrine on the first day of the new year.

New Year's Eve

The New Year's Eve celebration begins with a meal of toshikoshi soba (buckwheat noodles). Like the kadomatsu, they symbolize long life. On national television, the Red and White Song Festival, Kohaku Uta Gassen, broadcasts popular songs from the previous year. Many people watch this while they wait for Joya-no-Kane, the tolling of the temple bells. At midnight, all Buddhist temples solemnly ring their bells 108 times to drive away the 108 sins of mankind. People travel to see the massive bells ring at Japan's most famous temples or watch the ceremonies on television. Many Japanese rise early on New Year's Day to see the year's first sunrise.

On New Year's Day, it is traditional to make a pilgrimage to a Shinto shrine or a Buddhist temple.

On January 4, priests at the Shimogamo Shinto Shrine play the year's first kemari game, a game similar to soccer dating back to the Nara Era (500's-600's).

Traditional Entertainment

The blustery winter winds common in Japan during the New Year's festival are ideal for tako-age (kite-flying). Children make or buy the kites. A card game called karuta is also popular at this time. On January 6, Tokyo's firemen celebrate their return to work with fantastic acrobatic performances atop ladders.

Korea

새해복 많이 받으세요

***The Korean New Year greeting** is "Say hay boke-mahn he pah du say oh."*

The janggu, or buk, is a drum that the Jishin Balpgi celebrants use.

KOREANS COUNT THEIR BIRTHDAYS BY THE NUMBER OF NEW YEARS that they have lived through. Because every person in Korea eats one bowl of ttokkuk, rice cake soup, on New Year's Day, you can ask someone their age by saying, "How many dishes of ttokkuk have you eaten?"

TRADITIONALLY, EACH KOREAN FAMILY BUYS A SPECIAL RICE STRAINER called a bok jo ri on New Year's Day and hangs it on the wall for good fortune.

At the start of the new year, many people play Yut, a game that evolved from ancient farming rituals. Participants throw four sticks into the air and watch how they land to determine their fortunes.

***A ritual called Jishin Balpgi** (stepping on the spirit of the earth) is held on the 15th day of the new month. Musicians play drums and gongs to cleanse villages of evil spirits. They eat rice cakes and drink wine with the villagers.*

In Korea, respect for one's family and ancestors plays a central role in honoring the New Year. The Korean Lunar New Year, known as Seol, is celebrated on the first day of the first month of the new lunar year. It also marks the start of spring. Many Koreans celebrate the official New Year's Day, January 1, as well as the traditional lunar New Year's Day. On New Year's Eve, people prepare special foods and clean their houses. The house lights burn throughout the night, and everyone stays awake to greet New Year's Day, Seollal. In the morning, people dress in their best clothes. They make special food offerings to their ancestors in exchange for household blessings and say greetings to elders. Afterward, people enjoy celebratory breakfasts, visits with neighbors, games, fortune-telling, and dancing.

New Year's Morning

Seollal, New Year's Day, begins with a ceremony called Charye, to honor ancestors. Each family arranges an altar table carefully laid with special foods. The family's leader conducts the ritual, while someone else reads the chuk mun, a list of ancestors' names. After Charye, the children perform Sebae, the year's first formal greeting. They bow deeply to their parents and grandparents, and say, "Say hay boke-mahn he pah du say oh," which means "Please receive New Year's blessings." Afterward, the children receive money and cakes, and everyone enjoys an elaborate breakfast.

Thailand

Thailand's New Year's festival, Songkran, is the start of the Buddhist new year. It is an occasion for honoring local temples and elders and a cause for spirited celebration in the streets. Songkran falls on April 13, 14, and 15. During Songkran, people dress in traditional costumes for a ceremony to honor their elders with sprinklings of delicately scented water. Water, all-important for Thailand's agriculture, symbolizes renewal. People carefully cleanse Buddhist images with water during Songkran. Traditional water rituals have recently inspired more frenzied water-splashings in the streets, and people now enthusiastically drench everyone, including strangers. On April 14, people honor monks with gifts of food, new robes, and more sprinklings of fragrant water. Thai people also build stupas (dome-shaped monuments) of sand in temple courtyards. In the old days, Songkran was held at the end of the rainy season, and the stupas raised the temple's ground level.

A passing car is splashed during Songkran. People use buckets, pots, water pistols, and garden hoses to soak everyone they see.

This fish icon is an auspicious symbol for Thailand's new year. During Songkran, Thai people perform acts of merit, such as releasing trapped fish and caged birds, to receive blessings in return.

Rot Naam Dam Hua

In the ceremony of Rot Naam Dam Hua, younger family members pay respect to older relatives on New Year's Day. This ancient custom requires children to offer jasmine-and-spice-scented water with salutations to their elders, while asking for their forgiveness for misbehavior during the past year. In return, the elders apologize for the past year's punishments and give their children blessings and words of wisdom.

The Hill Tribes Celebrate

Thailand's hill tribes live in the remote northern region known as the Golden Triangle. Their ancestors, who originated in southern China and Tibet, migrated through neighboring Laos and Burma to Thailand in the early 1900's. These people remain committed to their traditional rural lifestyles, despite the influences of modern society. For them, New Year's Day is extremely important, as it marks the start of a new farming cycle. It can occur any time between early January and mid-February, according to each hill tribe's customs. Thailand has six hill tribes, each with its own cultural identity, rituals, religion, and distinctive clothing. They are the Lisu, the Karen, the Hmong, the Akha, the Mien, and the Lahu. During the New Year's celebrations, people try to impress each other by dressing in their best clothing and ornaments.

Hmong girls wear their best clothing and jewelry on New Year's Day. Some dress in skirts of indigo-blue cloth and leggings. Some Hmong wear white skirts. Over this, they wear embroidered aprons tied with red sashes, intricately batiked bibs, and silver necklaces.

This multi-colored silk turban is the traditional style of headdress for Lisu tribesmen during the New Year's festivities.

Akha women display their finery on New Year's Day. The Akha women wear elaborate headdresses, like the ones shown here decorated with silver coins, buttons, and beads, not only for celebrations, but every day.

Clothing and Jewelry

Women work for months to create the finest clothes possible for every member of their family to wear on New Year's Day. The Karen create beautifully embroidered cloth. The Mien women wear black turbans and red ruffs. Unmarried women and men dress the most extravagantly. Among the Hmong, Mien, Lahu, Lisu, and Akha tribespeople, silver symbolizes wealth and status. Many people display all their silver on New Year's Day to establish their family's position in the community and to attract partners for young, unmarried men and women.

These musical gourd pipes were made by Lahu people.

Lahu Celebrations

On New Year's morning, all families in a Lahu village exchange rice then cook rice cakes from the resulting mix. Each family then places some cakes on a household altar to ask for blessings. Villagers exchange gifts, spin tops, and play games. The entire village dances around the pine or bamboo year tree, which represents the holy, immortal Tree of Life. People draw fresh water to cleanse the hands of the other villagers and ask for blessings. They make offerings to the male and female gods for good health, a strong harvest, and many new children in the new year. The festival lasts for several days.

These women of the Lahu tribe sway in their traditional New Year's dance. The dancing is led by a man playing his ceremonial gourd pipe. Other musicians beat drums, gongs, and cymbals. The melodies of the pipe correspond to dance steps. All men, women, and children dance around the village's special year tree in a show of community spirit.

Lisu Celebrations

During the New Year's holiday, Lisu families compete with each other by wearing masses of silver jewelry. The Lisu religion, which combines ancestor worship with a belief in protective and harmful spirits, is also central to events. The village priest announces the end of the previous year, and he and the villagers plant their New Year's trees. Then the priest—the village's link to the spirit world—goes into a trance to drive away evil spirits. Young people dance around the New Year's trees to chase evil away. The next day, people take offerings to the village water source, cleanse themselves, and return to dance around the priest's tree.

This Lisu collar is the work of many weeks. The weaver first wove the brightly colored cloth, then created and attached the silver dangles one by one.

Preparing for Diwali

Diwali lamps are called diyas. Cotton strips are rolled and placed in small clay containers filled with oil. The diyas are lit and placed all over the house during Diwali.

South and Central Asia

In October or November, Hindus celebrate Diwali, the festival of lights. According to the ancient Hindu calendar, Diwali marks the beginning of the new year. Some Hindus also celebrate the god Rama's return from exile. For others, Diwali is the start of the new financial year, when they worship Lakshmi, the goddess of wealth. In East India and Bangladesh, Diwali honors the goddess Durga, who killed an evil buffalo demon. Diwali is also an important festival for Sikhs who remember the release from prison of Guru Hargobind in the 1600's. Diyas (oil lamps) are lit to guide the Guru back home. However Diwali is celebrated, its main message— the triumph of good over evil— is the same.

The flower sellers do a brisk business selling colorful garlands, above, by the dozen for decorating temples and homes. Traditionally, Hindus offer garlands to the gods and guests as a sign of welcome.

New Beginnings

Two days before Diwali, people give their homes a thorough cleaning as a reminder that the festival marks the start of a new year and a time of new beginnings. In preparation for the new year, old and unwanted objects are thrown away, new clothes are made or bought, and outstanding debts are paid.

Celebrating the god Rama's return from exile, as depicted by this statue, is one purpose of Diwali.

SOUTH AND CENTRAL ASIA

South and Central Asia are areas of distinct cultures and peoples. These regions form an area at the base of Asia. Asia extends from Africa and Europe in the west to the Pacific Ocean in the east. The northernmost part of the continent is in the Arctic. In the south, Asia ends in the tropics near the equator. South Asia is made up of Afghanistan, Armenia, Bangladesh, Bhutan, India, the Maldives, Nepal, Pakistan, Sri Lanka, the Tibetan plateau in southwest China, and parts of the countries of Azerbaijan and Georgia. Much of India, the largest country in south Asia, forms a peninsula that extends southward into the Indian Ocean. Central Asia includes the countries of Kazakhstan, Kyrgyzstan, Tajikistan, Turkmenistan, Uzbekistan, and the West Siberian Plain.

The Story of Rama

In northern India, Diwali celebrates the return of the popular Hindu god Rama to the kingdom of Ayodhya. His story is told in the *Ramayana*, one of the most sacred Hindu texts. Prince Rama is heir to his father's throne, but his jealous step-mother banishes him to the forest. There Rama's wife, Sita, is kidnapped by the evil demon king, Ravana. With the help of the monkey god, Hanuman, Rama rescues Sita and returns in triumph to Ayodhya. There he claims his rightful throne after 14 years in exile.

Burning Lamps

During Diwali, homes and temples are decorated with tiny diyas or candles. Traditionally, diyas are clay pots filled with mustard oil. Today, strings of electric lights are also hung across the streets. The lights are intended to welcome the goddess Lakshmi and to light Rama and Sita's way home. They are placed in rows along windowsills and all around the house. All the diyas are lit from the first diya lit on the first day of Diwali. The first diya is usually lit by the oldest person in the family.

Fireworks Displays

For days before Diwali, the streets are lined with stalls selling fireworks. Dazzling fireworks displays are an important part of Diwali festivities. The fireworks are set off on the evening of the second day, after family puja (prayers), in order to ward off evil. Many of the fireworks have pictures of the goddess Lakshmi emblazoned on them.

In Kolkata, a mother lights candles with her son at Diwali.

THE NAME *DIWALI* comes from the word *Deepavali*, which means row of lights.

HAPPY DIWALI! Many Hindus send Diwali cards to their friends and family. Shops have hundreds of intricate designs called rangoli patterns to choose from. The cards are decorated with the main Diwali themes, such as diyas and pictures of the goddess Lakshmi.

RANGOLI PATTERNS

- uncooked rice
- food coloring of various colors
- paper and pencil
- glue

Dye some rice by mixing it with food coloring. Dry the rice. Draw a pattern on a sheet of paper. (You can copy the designs on this page or create your own by combining simple shapes and coloring them in.) Trace the lines of the design with glue, then sprinkle the colored rice on the glue. You also can use colored chalk to draw a rangoli design on the sidewalk or on your doorstep.

Celebrating Diwali

In India, Diwali lasts for five days. Each day has its own customs and rituals. On the first day, Hindus make an offering to Yama, the god of death. On the second day, they remember the victory of the god Krishna over the terrible demon, Naraka. The third day of Diwali is called Lakshmi Puja. In the evening, families gather to say puja (prayers) in honor of the goddess Lakshmi. This is also the start of the new business year. The fourth day of Diwali is for worshiping the god Vishnu and remembering his victory over a tyrannical king. People also remember the god Krishna, who lifted up a mountain to shelter local villagers from a terrible storm. The last day of Diwali is called Bhaiya Dooj, when brothers visit their sisters' homes.

On the first day of Diwali, *Hindus light a lamp and place it with its flame pointing south as an offering to Yama, the god of death,* above. *This reminds them that death is part of life.*

Lakshmi

The third day of Diwali is dedicated to Lakshmi, the four-armed goddess of wealth and good fortune. In pictures, Lakshmi is shown standing or sitting in a lotus flower. In two of her hands, she holds lotus flowers, symbols of purity. The upraised palm of her third hand protects devotees from evil. Gold coins fall from her fourth hand, a sign of riches.

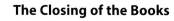

The Closing of the Books

For business people, Diwali marks the settling of old accounts and the beginning of a new financial year. In the mandir (temple) or at home, people place a pile of coins on top of their old account books and dedicate them to Lakshmi.

Performing Puja

At Diwali, many Hindus visit the mandir (temple) to say puja (prayers) and honor the gods and goddesses. The mandir is believed to be the god's home on Earth. A sacred image represents the god's presence. Worshipers recite verses from the sacred texts and make offerings of diyas, food, and flower garlands in return for the gods' blessings. Puja is also performed at home in a room or part of a room set aside for that purpose.

Bhaiya Dooj

The last day of Diwali is called Bhaiya Dooj. This is a day for brothers to visit their sisters' homes and enjoy a delicious Diwali meal. This tradition is a reminder of how Yama, the god of death, visited his sister on this day and ate a special meal. In return, brothers promise to look after and protect their sisters. They also take their sisters a present of jewelry, money, or clothes.

Sweet Treats

At every Hindu festival there is special food to eat. Boxes of sweets made from milk, coconut, sugar, and nuts are given as gifts to friends and relatives. People make sweets at home or buy them from sweet shops. Piles of puffed rice, called khil, are also popular at Diwali.

Sisters, like these two girls from Bombay, are celebrated by their brothers on the last day of Diwali.

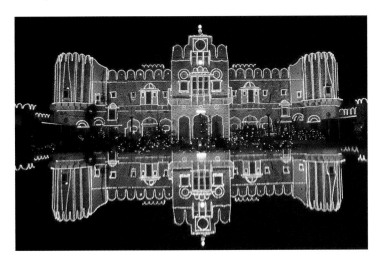

City Lights

During Diwali, homes, schools, and offices all over India are decorated with bright lights. In Jaipur, a city in western India, the main markets, streets, and squares are lit up for the entire festival. Prizes are awarded for the most dazzling displays. In some towns and villages, there is also a mela (fair). Stalls sell clothes, bangles, and spicy snacks. Acrobats, jugglers, and fortunetellers entertain the crowds.

Ganpati Plaza in Jaipur, far left, regularly wins the prize for best Diwali illuminations!

Sticky, sweet besan laddus, left, are sold at Diwali. The sweets are piled up in pyramid shapes and sold on the streets.

This silk apron is traditionally worn during the sacred Cham dance. An image of Mahakala, one of the eight Guardians of the Faith, is depicted in the center.

BUDDHA means Enlightened One and is the title given to the founder of Buddhism, one of the world's great religions. Buddha's name was Siddhartha Gautama.

THE DALAI LAMA, Tibet's religious leader, now lives in exile in India. To wish him a happy new year, the three great monasteries in Tibet offer him a special barley cake.

Losar

The Tibetan New Year is celebrated in February or March with the festival of Losar. This is a happy time for visiting friends and family and remembering the life of Buddha. It is also a time to leave bad luck and negative thoughts behind and herald in a good new year. Losar celebrations begin a few days before New Year's Day. Houses and monasteries are cleaned and decorated, new clothes are made, and old quarrels settled. On New Year's Day, people get up early and collect water from the river or well. Water collected on this day is thought to be particularly lucky. Before the Chinese invasion of Tibet in the 1950's, Losar celebrations lasted for 15 days, and huge crowds gathered in the monasteries. Today, Tibetan refugees in Nepal and India usually celebrate for 3 days.

Tormas are offerings made from barley flour dough and covered with sculptures made from yak butter. Huge tormas are made by Tibetan monks for festivals such as Losar. The decorations include lucky symbols, heavenly beings, and scenes from Buddha's life.

These masked dancers are performing the Cham in skeleton-lord costume.

Cham Dances

Festivals and special occasions in Tibet were traditionally marked by performances of the colorful sacred dance called Cham. These dances were held in the courtyards of the great monasteries. The dances always include certain characters dressed in elaborate costumes and vivid masks. Among them are Yama, the god of death; his stag-headed messenger; the Black Hat priest; and the skeleton lords. The dances are intended to drive out the bad luck of the old year and ensure a good start to the new one.

The Dalai Lama blesses an offering. In the background is a huge pile of khapse.

Festival Foods

Special foods are eaten at Losar, such as khapse (fried pastries). These are also placed on the family altar. On New Year's Eve, the family eats dumpling soup, called gutuk. The dumplings are stuffed with special ingredients that predict what the new year will bring. If you find salt inside, you'll have good luck; if you find coal, it means a bad year.

New Prayer Flags

In Tibet, brightly colored prayer flags flutter from the rooftop of every home and monastery. The flags have hundreds of prayers written on them. Each time the wind blows, it carries the prayers into the world. At Losar, the old prayer flags are taken down and replaced with new ones.

Throwing Tsampa

Throwing tsampa (roasted barley flour) into the air is an important Losar custom. In people's homes, guests are presented with a pot of tsampa. They take a pinch and throw it into the air to honor Buddha and bring good fortune. Tsampa is a staple of the Tibetan diet and is often eaten mixed with yak butter.

This Tibetan monk hoists new prayer flags during Losar.

Lamps filled with butter made from yak milk are lit at shrines and at monasteries during the festival.

New Year's Worship

At Losar, people visit the monasteries to pay their respects to Buddha and make offerings of khatas (white greeting scarves), food, and donations to the monks. Devotees bow or kneel before the image of Buddha and light yak-butter lamps. The monks chant from the sacred texts and burn bundles of sweet-smelling juniper and cedar branches.

At Losar, people visit the monasteries and throw handfuls of tsampa into the air to welcome in the new year and attract good luck.

The pomegranate is one of seven sacred fruits of the land of Israel. It is eaten during Rosh Ha-Shanah because of its crownlike top, which symbolizes God's kingdom.

The Middle East

Rosh Ha-Shanah

Rosh Ha-Shanah is a solemn yet joyful occasion when Jewish people repent to God for their sins and celebrate their future redemption. *Rosh Ha-Shanah* means beginning of the year in Hebrew. The new religious year starts on the first day of the first month of the Hebrew calendar, sometime between mid-September and early October on the Gregorian calendar. According to the sacred Talmud, God decides everyone's fate during this holy time. On the two days of Rosh Ha-Shanah, God writes the names of truly virtuous people in the Book of Life, and those of wholly wicked people in the Book of Death. Everyone else's fate is determined during the following period known as the Ten Days of Penitence, when Jews make amends and repent for the previous year's sins. This period ends with Yom Kippur, the Day of Atonement.

The Shofar
The Torah, the holy scripture of Judaism, refers to Rosh Ha-Shanah as "a day of sounding the shofar." *Shofar* is the Hebrew word for a trumpet made from an animal's horn, usually a ram's. On each day of Rosh Ha-Shanah, 100 notes blown from a shofar call the people to repent.

Rosh Ha-Shanah
Yom Kippur

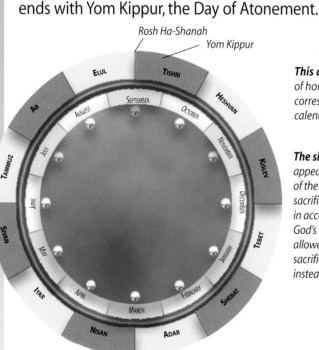

This diagram gives a general idea of how the Hebrew calendar corresponds to the Gregorian calendar in A.D. 2003.

The shofar recalls the ram that appeared before Abraham, patriarch of the Jews, as he prepared to sacrifice his son Isaac in accordance with God's will. God allowed Abraham to sacrifice the ram instead.

THE MIDDLE EAST

The Middle East covers parts of northern Africa, southwestern Asia, and southeastern Europe. Scholars disagree on which countries make up the Middle East. But many say the region consists of Bahrain, Cyprus, Egypt, Iran, Iraq, Israel, Jordan, Kuwait, Lebanon, Oman, Qatar, Saudi Arabia, Sudan, Syria, Turkey, United Arab Emirates, and Yemen. The region also is the birthplace of three major religions—Judaism, Christianity, and Islam.

The Hebrew Calendar
The Hebrew calendar, now in its 58th century, is the oldest calendar still in use for religious and civil purposes. It is a lunar calendar, and includes 12 months in a regular year, and 13 months in a leap year. To keep it in line with the solar calendar, a month called Veadar is added between the months of Adar and Nisan 7 times every 19 years. Hebrew years vary in length, from 353 to 385 days, to achieve this.

CHALLAH

- 1 ¼ cups warm water
- ½ tablespoon active dry yeast
- 4–5 cups unbleached all-purpose flour
- ½ tablespoon salt
- ⅓ cup honey
- 2 tablespoons vegetable oil
- 3 eggs, lightly beaten
- ¾ cup golden raisins
- 2 tablespoons poppy seeds (optional)

Place 1 ¼ cup of warm water in a small bowl and sprinkle with the yeast. Set aside for 15 minutes. Place 4 cups of flour with the salt in a large bowl. Stir in the yeast mixture, followed by the honey, oil, and one-third of the egg. Mix well to obtain a thick kneadable dough, adding more flour if required. Turn onto a clean, lightly floured work surface and knead until smooth and elastic, adding flour as required. Cover with a clean cloth and let rise for 2 hours or until dough has doubled in bulk.

Turn the risen dough onto a floured surface and knead for about 5 minutes, adding the raisins and enough flour to stop the dough from sticking. Divide the dough into 3 pieces and roll each into a long snake about 1½ inches in diameter. Pinch the ends of the three snakes together firmly and braid them. Shape into a round loaf by bringing the ends around until they touch. Pinch them together. Grease a baking sheet and place the loaf on it. Cover with a towel and let rise for 1 hour. Preheat oven to 375 °F. Brush with the remaining egg and sprinkle with poppy seeds. Bake for about 40 minutes. Cool on a rack for 1 hour before slicing.

Rosh Ha-Shanah Foods

On the first night of Rosh Ha-Shanah, families eat special foods that represent hopes for the coming year. Circular challah bread represents the cycle of the year. In an old tradition, a whole fish, including the head, was placed before the family patriarch to show his position as head of the family. People avoid eating bitter foods, and some avoid nuts because the Hebrew word for nut is similar to the word for sin.

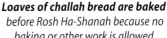

Challah bread, wine, and candles are reverently presented for the evening meal on the first night of *Rosh Ha-Shanah,* right.

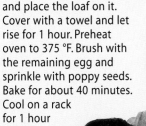

Loaves of challah bread are baked before Rosh Ha-Shanah because no baking or other work is allowed on the Jewish holy day itself, left.

Forbidden Work

According to a section of the Torah, work is forbidden during Rosh Ha-Shanah. Prohibited work includes driving, writing, handling money, and any activities related to one's own occupation. People must cook, bake, carry objects, and tend fires before the holidays to prepare the special Rosh Ha-Shanah and Yom Kippur foods. Many Jewish people also avoid most of these types of work on regular Sabbath days.

PEOPLE EAT APPLES DIPPED IN HONEY on Rosh Ha-Shanah to symbolize their hopes for a good and sweet new year.

The Torah *is the Hebrew name for Judaism's most important scriptures. Jews believe that God gave the Torah directly to Moses, their ancestor. They must use a special pointer called a yad when reading from it.*

New Year's Worship

This silver chalice *was made for Kiddush.*

Worship is central to the observance of Rosh Ha-Shanah, the time when Jews renew their commitment to their faith and reverence for God and His laws. Rosh Ha-shanah is a time when Jewish people recall and celebrate the creation of the world. The holiday begins at sunset. Jewish families light candles and consume bread and wine while reciting a blessing called Kiddush. The family patriarch leads the ceremony and recites a prayer of thankfulness. The next day, everyone worships together in a synagogue, praying and attending to the special service. During Rosh Ha-Shanah and Yom Kippur, rabbis offer special prayers and readings. Throughout the holy period, Jewish people also pray alone to God for forgiveness, obedience, and redemption.

This beautifully decorated silver case holds a mahzor, which is a special book with prayers, hymns, and Bible readings for each holy day in the Jewish calendar.

FOR JEWISH PEOPLE THE NEW DAY always begins at sunset. For this reason, Jewish festivals, including the New Year's holiday, all begin in the evening.

This family is making a toast at a festive meal during Rosh Ha-Shanah. Rosh Ha-Shanah occurs during the autumn, when people enjoy the fruits of the harvest. Several of its rituals involve foods. The first night of Rosh Ha-Shanah, each family gathers for a meal and offers thankful prayers.

Tashlikh

Many Jews observe the ritual of Tashlikh on the first day of Rosh Ha-Shanah. This ritual evolved from certain passages in the Bible, such as, "You will cast all their sins into the depths of the sea." To perform Tashlikh, worshipers visit a river, stream, or ocean and ceremonially toss pieces of bread, representing sins, into the water. Then they offer penitential prayers. Tashlikh demonstrates how God's forgiveness will wash away sins.

Yom Kippur

Yom Kippur, the Day of Atonement, is the holiest day of the year for Jewish people. On Yom Kippur, God passes final judgments on the righteousness and wickedness of each person, having considered their repentance and prayers during the days of penitence. God inscribes each Jew's name in either the Book of Life or the Book of Death. These inscriptions are sealed and unchangeable until the next Yom Kippur. Because Yom Kippur is the last chance to repent and change God's judgment, people spend the day in solemn prayer. Starting at sunset the night before, they refrain from eating and drinking for 25 hours. This fast symbolizes purification of the body and spirit. Everyone attends synagogue and recites the Kol Nidrei, an appeal for God's forgiveness of their sins, plus additional prayers and Torah readings. At sunset, the shofar sounds and Yom Kippur ends with the breaking of the fast.

During prayer, Jewish males wear a head covering called a yarmulka or skullcap. It is a symbol of one's humility before God. The yarmulka is also worn on special occasions, such as religious ceremonies and the Sabbath. Some Jewish males wear their yarmulkas all the time.

Traditions and Prohibitions

During Yom Kippur, Jewish people concentrate on the spiritual and eternal aspects of their existence. Activities prohibited during Yom Kippur include eating, drinking, washing, applying lotions to the skin, sexual relations, and wearing leather shoes. People who are ill, pregnant, younger than 13, or very old are forbidden to fast. These religious laws come from the Talmud, the Jewish holy scriptures that outline laws, customs, and interpretations of the Torah. The Talmud developed between A.D. 70 and 500.

This boy is performing the kapparot ceremony.
Special verses from the Yom Kippur mahzor prayer book are recited, and a chicken is waved over one's head. It is believed that one's sins from the past year are transferred to the chicken. After the ceremony, the chicken is slaughtered and given to charity.

At sunset as Yom Kippur begins, Jewish women light Yahrzeit candles. As these candles are lit, family members ask each other for forgiveness for any wrongdoing in the previous year.

Tu B'Shevat

The New Year for Trees occurs on the 15th day of Shebat (Tu B'Shebat) on the Hebrew calendar, which falls in late January or early February on the Gregorian calendar. Jewish families plant trees, particularly fruit trees. In Israel, children wear wreaths of flowers and plant saplings. Many Sephardic, or Middle Eastern, Jews celebrate Tu B'Shevat by eating the seven "fruits" of Israel: wheat, barley, grapes, figs, pomegranates, olives, and dates, or by holding a special seder—a ritual meal with prayers—at home.

These children are planting young trees for the festival of Tu B' Shebat. In Israel, Tu B' Shebat is a national environmental holiday on which people help reforestation projects.

Hijra

The first day of the month of Muharram is the beginning of the Muslim year. Hijra, the Muslim New Year, commemorates the flight of the Prophet Muhammad and his followers from Mecca to Medina in A.D. 622, and the founding of the first Islamic community there. The entire month of Muharram is a holy month. There are fast days, processions, and gatherings in mosques for prayers. The first 10 days are observed as a period of mourning, especially by Shiah Muslims. The 10th of Muharram, Ashura, is a particularly important day for them. There are public displays of great sorrow, as they remember the martyrdom of Muhammad's grandson, Husayn.

Devout Muslims pray five times daily, wherever they are. Many attend the mosque for Friday prayers and on festivals.

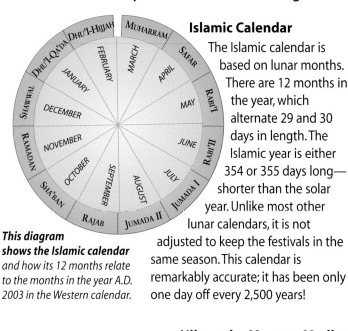

This diagram shows the Islamic calendar and how its 12 months relate to the months in the year A.D. 2003 in the Western calendar.

Islamic Calendar

The Islamic calendar is based on lunar months. There are 12 months in the year, which alternate 29 and 30 days in length. The Islamic year is either 354 or 355 days long—shorter than the solar year. Unlike most other lunar calendars, it is not adjusted to keep the festivals in the same season. This calendar is remarkably accurate; it has been only one day off every 2,500 years!

This decorated tile depicts the city of Medina and the temple area.

Hijra—the Move to Medina

The Prophet Muhammad was born in Mecca in A.D. 570. Muslims believe Muhammad began to receive revelations from Allah in about A.D. 610. Allah is the Arabic name for the Supreme Being of the religion of Islam. Muhammad began to teach people that they should worship one god instead of many. The rulers of Mecca saw Muhammad's teachings as a threat, so in A.D. 622 he and his followers moved to Medina.

Today, Muslims live throughout the world. This map shows only those areas where the majority of people are Muslims. It also shows areas that are mainly Sunni (in yellow) and those that are mainly Shiah (in pink).

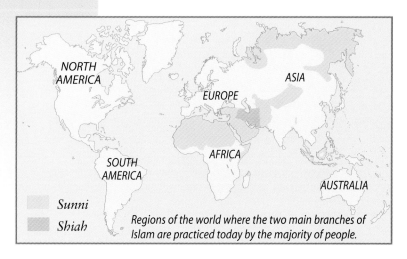

Sunni

Shiah

Regions of the world where the two main branches of Islam are practiced today by the majority of people.

Islam Around the World

In Mecca, Muhammad established Islamic rule. After his death, Islam spread quickly through the Middle East, North Africa, and Asia, also reaching West Africa and southeastern Europe. Today, there are two main branches of Islam. After the Prophet died, some Muslims wanted to choose their leaders; they became the Sunnis. Others, who became known as Shiah Muslims, believed their leaders should come from the family of the Prophet. They were devastated when the Prophet's grandson, Husayn, was killed by the followers of the Muslim ruler Yazid.

Muharram

The new year begins when the new moon is sighted. Muharram is one of the four sacred months mentioned in the Quran (also spelled Koran). At New Year's, Muslims make a fresh start. They try to put behind them any bad actions they might have done and resolve to do things better in the new year. There are religious gatherings and processions from the beginning of the month, becoming larger from the seventh of Muharram.

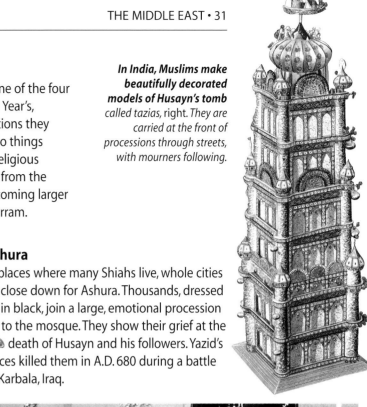

In India, Muslims make beautifully decorated models of Husayn's tomb called tazias, right. *They are carried at the front of processions through streets, with mourners following.*

Ashura

In places where many Shiahs live, whole cities close down for Ashura. Thousands, dressed in black, join a large, emotional procession to the mosque. They show their grief at the death of Husayn and his followers. Yazid's forces killed them in A.D. 680 during a battle at Karbala, Iraq.

During the Battle of Karbala, illustrated above, the grandson of Muhammad, Husayn, was killed.

Grief over Husayn

As part of their mourning, Muslims fast on Ashura. Some particularly devout Shiah men march in the Ashura procession with bare chests; they may beat or even cut themselves. This serves to help them share the sufferings of the martyrs. Everyone in the procession chants "Ya Husayn" and wails in sorrow. There is usually a beautifully decorated white horse in the procession, in memory of Husayn's horse, left without its rider after his martyrdom. Scenes from the battle at Karbala are acted out.

At the Mosque

At Hijra, Muslims gather in the mosque to pray and hear about the life and sacrifices of the Prophet Muhammad and his early followers. At Ashura, they hear about the battle of Karbala and the death of Husayn and his followers. Husayn and his followers were deprived of food and water while under siege. In their memory, Shiah Muslims set up drinking posts, offering free water and juice to the faithful.

These Muslims are praying in the Blue Mosque in Istanbul, Turkey.

In a procession at Ashura, men hold whips with which they either symbolically or actually beat themselves.

Queen Elizabeth I (1533–1603) demanded gifts from her English subjects on New Year's Day. She kept lists of the gifts she received. King Henry III (1207–1272) had started this tradition, which ended in the 1600's.

Europe and the Americas

European Traditions

Many of today's New Year's traditions in Europe are centuries old. The fire ceremonies and parades held in Britain, Switzerland, and elsewhere originated with the Celts, who dominated many areas of Europe before their conquest by the Roman Empire. The Vikings added their midwinter Yule customs to European culture. The ancient Roman calendar gave the Western world its official date for New Year's Day, January 1 (see page 9). In Greece today, the New Year's festival coincides with the centuries-old celebration of St. Basil's Day, which honors a founder of the Eastern Orthodox Church.

Hogmanay

New Year's Eve in Scotland is called Hogmanay. The word *Hogmanay* may come from the Gaelic term *oge maidne,* which means new morning. Today, the Scots enjoy Hogmanay street parties and ceilidhs (pronounced kay lihs), gatherings for dancing, singing, and storytelling. According to a tradition called first footing, the appearance of a dark-haired stranger on your doorstep at midnight is considered good luck.

"Auld Lang Syne"

The Scottish poet Robert Burns transcribed the traditional song "Auld Lang Syne" in 1788. In the Scots dialect, the title means old long since or days gone by. Now, English-speaking people everywhere link arms and sing it on New Year's Eve.

The bagpipes are a musical instrument played in Scotland and other countries. Proud pipers greet the new year with gusto in Scotland and around the world.

EUROPE

Europe is one of the smallest of the world's seven continents in area but one of the largest in population. Europe extends from the Arctic Ocean in the north to the Mediterranean Sea in the south and from the Atlantic Ocean in the west to the Ural Mountains in the east. The 47 countries of Europe include the world's largest country, Russia, as well as the world's smallest, Vatican City. Russia lies partly in Europe and partly in Asia.

Fire Ceremonies

Many Hogmanay traditions can be traced back to ancient pagan (pre-Christian) times. The original inhabitants of Scotland worshiped the sun. Hogmanay occurs during darkest winter. People traditionally celebrated the sun's arrival—and the approaching sunnier days—by lighting fires. Today, Scottish people hold torchlight processions, light bonfires, and watch fireworks.

Dressing up in traditional Viking costume to celebrate Hogmanay has become part of the fun in Scotland.

ST. BASIL'S CAKE—VASILOPITTA

- 10 eggs
- 1 cup butter or margarine
- 3 cups granulated sugar
- 2 tablespoons vanilla sugar
- 4 tablespoons brandy (optional)
- juice and zest of 4 oranges
- 5 cups self-rising flour
- 1 large coin wrapped in aluminum foil
- $^1/_2$ cup walnuts or sesame seeds

Separate the egg yolks from the whites. Beat the whites until stiff. In a bowl, beat the butter and sugar with egg yolks and vanilla sugar until light and creamy. Fold whites into this mixture. Add the brandy, if using, orange juice, and zest. Gradually sift the flour into the mixture and mix until smooth. Add the coin. Spoon the batter into a round, greased cake pan. Sprinkle with the sesame seeds or walnuts. Bake at 350 °F for about 1 hour.

St. Basil the Great (A.D. 330?–379) *renounced his earthly possessions and lived in great poverty while defending the Orthodox Christian faith. He is renowned today for his love of the poor and his kindness to children.*

New Year's in Greece

New Year's Day, January 1, is also the Festival of St. Basil, an early leader of the Eastern Orthodox Church. Greeks visit their friends and family and enjoy great feasts, singing, and dancing. Children leave their shoes by the fireplace for "St. Basil" to fill with gifts. Families buy or prepare a special St. Basil's Cake called Vasilopitta (see recipe, *above*), which contains a large gold or silver coin. Each person in the house gets one piece of cake—including, ceremonially, St. Basil— and whoever receives the coin can expect good luck throughout the new year.

New Year's Beliefs

Throughout Europe, many New Year's Day customs involve eating particular foods to ensure good luck, wealth, and happiness during the coming year. Germans, Austrians, and Hungarians eat pork to bring wealth. Greeks and Bulgarians eat honey for a sweet and happy new year. Other lucky foods include donuts in the Netherlands and lentils in Italy. In Scotland, people traditionally offer shortbread and whisky to their "first footers" (see page 32). Other traditions involve destroying old objects. In Denmark, people smash old dishes to clear the way for the next year.

At midnight on New Year's Eve in Spain, people eat 12 grapes in time with each of the 12 chimes from clocks in Madrid, the capital, and elsewhere around the country. This is difficult and comical. Some say the tradition started one New Year's Eve when a king gave grapes to his subjects to celebrate a good harvest.

Masks like this one are used to chase away evil spirits during the Achetringele celebrations held in small villages in Switzerland.

Achetringele

The Celts of what is now Switzerland started the tradition of Achetringele, which the Swiss still observe in some smaller villages. At the winter solstice, the ancient Celts chased evil spirits from their villages by ringing bells and wearing fierce masks. Today, Achetringele takes place on New Year's Eve. Three different masked groups march through the village: bell ringers; broom-sweepers; and men carrying pigs' bladders filled with air. The marchers destroy fake weapons carried by observers as they parade by.

Celebrating in Europe

The Dutch like to drink hot, spicy wine on New Year's Eve. They also eat large meals with family and friends. Donuts, above, are often served in Dutch homes on New Year's Day. The treats are believed to bring good luck in the new year.

New Year's Day is celebrated throughout Europe in many different ways. Some customs are related to age-old folk traditions and pagan (pre-Christian) festivities, when people celebrated the turning point of the winter solstice and their joy at the lengthening of the days, as spring approached. In many countries, these traditions have mingled with Christian festivals marking saints' days, such as the Orthodox Christian St. Basil's Day in Greece and Bulgaria. However, many traditional festivals are dying out as more people spend New Year's Eve in front of the television or with groups of friends and family eating, drinking, and making merry.

At the Stroke of Midnight

In cities all over Europe, people gather in the streets to bring in the new year. They count down the seconds until the start of the new year. At the stroke of midnight, the crowds cheer, blow horns, and make a lot of noise. Elaborate fireworks displays light up the sky, and in some countries, church bells ring. Celebrations go on through the night during the biggest party of the year.

Drummers in colorful costumes march in a parade through the streets of Paris.

DINNER PARTIES, BALLS, AND SOCIAL EVENTS

In Vienna, Austria, the new year is celebrated with a special concert by the Vienna Philharmonic Orchestra. Tickets are almost impossible to get unless you belong to certain families who pass them on from generation to generation. However, since 1959, people from around the world have been able to enjoy the concert because it has been televised. The New Year's concert in Vienna features Viennese waltz music, especially "The Blue Danube." In the past, people danced at New Year's balls until dawn.

St. Peter's Basilica in Vatican City in Italy holds mass on New Year's Day.

WHEN WALTZING FIRST BECAME POPULAR in European capitals in the 1800's, it was considered scandalous for a young, unmarried lady to waltz in public with men with whom she was not formally acquainted.

St. Basil's Day in Bulgaria

New Year's Day in Bulgaria is called St. Basil's Day. It is celebrated on January 1. On New Year's Eve in traditional homes, the entire family gathers to eat a large meal. Dishes include pig's head and jellied pig's feet, served with walnuts, honey, wine, and brandy. A round loaf with a silver coin inside is served at the end of the meal. Whoever gets the coin will enjoy a healthy and wealthy new year.

Grandfather Frost

Because Russia uses two calendars—Julian and Gregorian—there are many holidays at this time of year. Russians celebrate December 25 and January 1 as well as January 7 (Orthodox Christmas) and January 14 (Orthodox New Year). In Russia, Ded Moroz—Grandfather Frost—bearing gifts, visits homes on December 31 and January 1.

In Bulgarian villages, a special ceremony called sourvakari, above, *is eagerly awaited. Just before dawn, the village men go from house to house wishing everyone a happy new year. They tap everyone they meet on the back with a decorated twig and wish them health, longevity, and success.*

Grandfather Frost, above, *has a red-and-white fur-trimmed coat and long beard and looks much like Santa Claus. However, Russian children do not get their gifts automatically; they must sing, dance, or recite a poem to earn a gift.*

Malanka in the Ukraine

The Ukrainian folk festival called Malanka is celebrated on January 13, which is New Year's Eve according to the Julian calendar. On this night, Ukrainian villagers dress up as witches, soldiers, old men or women, musicians, or gypsies, or as other characters. They parade through the village acting out traditional songs, dances, and stories and improvising new ones. At about six in the morning, they go to bed for a few hours. Then the celebration begins again until sunset. The day finishes with a huge feast.

Malanka festivities combine Orthodox Christian feast days and the pre-Christian folk festivals that celebrated the passing of the longest days of winter.

United States and Canada

In Canada and the United States, where people come from many different religions and cultural backgrounds, New Year's Day is a celebration that everyone can share. Some festivities, such as the Mummers' Parade in Philadelphia, Pennsylvania, originated from a mix of cultural traditions brought over by immigrants—in this case, people from England, Sweden, Poland, and several African countries. A few practices, like the midnight dropping of the New Year's ball in New York City or eating black-eyed peas for good luck, began in the Americas.

In the United States, eating black-eyed peas on New Year's Day is believed to bring good fortune. Originally a staple in Southern States, black-eyed peas are served in both traditional and modern dishes. Serving greens with black-eyed peas is thought to bring wealth.

THE FIRST OFFICIAL MUMMERS' PARADE was held in 1901, but immigrants in south Philadelphia began taking to the streets to celebrate the new year in the 1880's. In 1901, the city government began sponsoring the parade and moved the route downtown, through the city center. During the 1940's, as many as 2 million spectators turned out to watch. Nowadays, about 250,000 people attend.

Many people in the United States watch the Tournament of Roses Parade and Rose Bowl football game, both held in Pasadena, California, on New Year's Day. The first parade, held in 1890, included rose-covered floats, followed by sports competitions.

Philadelphia's New Year's Day Mummers' Parade has evolved from several American immigrant traditions. Paraders wear comical masks and costumes, below, strut dramatically, and play in competing string bands.

Parades and Events

Lunch on New Year's Day may be a large feast with friends and family. Afterward, many people watch televised parades and football games, such as the Tournament of Roses Parade and Rose Bowl football game in California, the Mummers' Parade in Pennsylvania, the Orange Bowl Parade and football game in Florida, Texas's Cotton Bowl, and Louisiana's Sugar Bowl.

THE AMERICAS

The continents of North America and South America make up the Western Hemisphere. North America contains Canada, Greenland, the United States, Mexico, Central America, and the Caribbean Sea islands. South America contains Argentina, Bolivia, Brazil (which occupies almost half the continent), Chile, Colombia, Ecuador, Guyana, Paraguay, Peru, Suriname, Uruguay, and Venezuela.

ON NEW YEAR'S DAY, MANY PEOPLE MAKE LISTS of resolutions to keep better habits in the coming year.

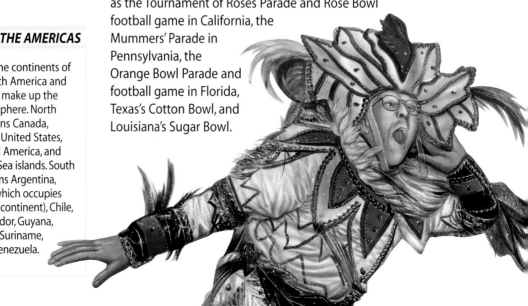

New Year's Eve in New York

The first New Year's Eve party in New York City's Times Square took place in 1904, when the owners of *The New York Times* newspaper celebrated their move to a new office building there. Today, millions watch the New Year's Eve ball, introduced in 1907, as it begins dropping just before midnight to usher in the new year. The ball is 6 feet in diameter and weighs about 1,070 pounds. The outside is covered with 504 crystal triangles and 168 light bulbs. Inside are 528 lights of varying colors. Rotating pyramid mirrors help create a spectacular light show.

New York City's New Year's Eve ball is 6 feet in diameter and weighs about 1,070 pounds. The outside is covered with crystal triangles and light bulbs.

Icy Dips

Some Canadian and American swimmers plunge into icy waters on New Year's Day. Polar Bear Clubs organize large group swims. Participants claim that the New Year's Day swim brings good luck and enables them to face the coming year with a sharp, clear mind.

Swimmers at Coney Island, New York, take the plunge on New Year's Day. They are all members of the local Polar Bear Club.

This carved buffalo head was placed on an altar during the Shalako ceremony at a village in the Southwest. The Zuni believe that certain animals and plants can help humans to communicate with the powers that control the universe.

The Shalako Ceremony

The Zuni people of the southwestern United States celebrate the arrival of the new year during the first week of December with Shalako. They prepare for the ceremony by building seven houses for the Shalako (giant messengers of the rainmakers) and the Longhorns (rain gods of the north). In the dry Southwest, the annual rains are essential. The two-day festivities consist of prayer, feasting, dancing, and the reenactment of Zuni myths. All are intended to bring rain in the new year, as well as ensure the health and good fortune of the participants.

The tradition of using an elderly man to symbolize the outgoing year dates back to ancient times. The ancient Greek harvest god Kronos evolved through the ages into our Father Time. Father Time is usually depicted with a long white beard and holding his scythe for harvesting.

Latin America

The Maya pyramid at Chichen Itza in Mexico is actually a calendar with 365 steps, one for each day of the year. The Maya civilization flourished in what is now known as Mexico from A.D. 250 to 900.

The countries of Central and South America have very rich cultural heritages. The customs of the indigenous peoples have mingled with those of the Spanish and Portuguese settlers who came after the 1500's, and of the many African peoples whose ancestors were brought to the region as slaves. The variety and richness of their customs are most apparent at New Year. People across the continent salute the parting year, usually by burning large male Año Viejo (Old Year) dolls, and greet the new year with street and beach parties, fireworks, feasting, music, dancing, and prayer.

NEW YEAR'S BELIEFS:

In Mexico and Venezuela, people eat 12 grapes, one for each chime of the clock as it strikes midnight. This custom comes from Spain.

In Venezuela, Mexico, and Ecuador, people who hope to travel in the coming year take their suitcases out and walk with them around the house or even around the block.

In Mexico, it is considered very bad luck to go down a ladder or ride in a red car on New Year's Day.

In Costa Rica, housewives prepare for New Year's Day by sweeping out the whole house. They believe that they are sweeping away the bad luck of the old year along with the dust and grime.

In Bolivia, people hang little wooden or straw dolls outside their homes for good luck.

Costa Rica

New Year's celebrations are part of the Christmas festivities that begin in mid-December and finish on January 6, the day on which the Wise Men traditionally found and worshiped the baby Jesus. During the last week of December, special events such as bullfights, horse processions, and dances are held and usually extend through the beginning of January.

The annual End-of-Year Parade meanders through the streets of San José, capital city of Costa Rica, on January 1. Brightly colored carts pulled by oxen accompany children dressed in traditional costumes.

GUACAMOLE

- 5 avocados
- 2 teaspoons lemon or lime juice
- 1/2 teaspoon salt
- 1 green onion
- 2 tablespoons green chili
- 2 cloves garlic
- 1/2 tomato

Cut the avocados in half lengthwise. Remove the stones. Use a spoon to scoop out the green, fleshy part of the avocados. Put the flesh into a bowl. Mash the avocado flesh using the back of a fork. Add the lemon juice and salt. Stir. Chop the green onion and the green chili. Peel and mince the garlic. Add the onion, garlic, and chilies to the avocado and stir well. Chop the tomato into small pieces. Add the pieces to the avocado and stir well. Place the guacamole in an attractive serving dish. Serve as a dip with tostadas or corn chips.

Mexico

Most Mexicans celebrate New Year's Day by getting together with family and friends. Preparations begin in the days leading up to New Year's Eve, as people clean their houses, shop, and cook for the feast days ahead. At midnight, people kiss each other, hug, and often raise a glass of champagne to toast the incoming year. Many go outside and watch the stars to welcome the new year. Some shoot guns and shout as the clock strikes midnight.

Traditional Foods

Tamales are a favorite New Year's dish in Mexico as well as many Central American countries. Traditional foods, such as posada, tortillas, salsa, mole, and guacamole (see recipe, *left*), are accompanied by beer, tequila, and ponche (hot fruit punch) for the adults and atole (a sweet, hot beverage made with ground corn) for the children.

People wear colored underwear on New Year's Eve for good luck. In Venezuela, Mexico, Brazil, and Colombia, yellow underwear is thought to ensure wealth. White is worn for peace, and red is worn for success in love. In Argentina, pink is the favored color for love. For some, extra luck can be gained by wearing the underwear inside out, while for others, this would ensure a disastrous new year!

New Year's in Brazil

In Brazil, people wear white clothes on New Year's Eve to bring good luck and peace in the coming year. Brazilians who live near a beach bring flowers, candles, and small statues down to the water after midnight. They each decorate part of the beach, light their candles, and wait for the tide to come in and wash their ornaments away. This is thought to bring good luck in the new year. A great feast follows.

San Juan Chamula, built in the 1500's by Dominican missionaries, is the most deeply respected sanctuary of the Tzotzil people of the Chiapas in Mexico.

MINGLED RELIGIOUS TRADITIONS

Most Central and South Americans are Roman Catholics. Catholicism was taken to the region by Portuguese and Spanish colonialists beginning in the late 1400's. But Christianity has mingled with the traditions of the native people and of Africans brought there as slaves. Many of the people who attend mass also take part in beach ceremonies dedicated to the goddess of the sea, a tradition probably of African origin.

Año Viejo Dolls in South America

In many Latin American countries, people cast off the old year by creating life-sized Año Viejo (Old Year) dolls and burning them at midnight on New Year's Eve. The Año Viejo dolls are stuffed with sawdust or eucalyptus, dressed in old clothes, and decorated with elaborate masks. Sometimes fireworks are added to the stuffing to make it more exciting as it burns. The dolls represent terrible events or people who brought sadness to a family or community. As the Año Viejo dolls are destroyed, so are any bad memories of the past year.

This Año Viejo mask comes from Mexico. In some countries, children prepare the masks and dolls days before New Year's Day and charge family, friends, and passersby for the privilege of viewing them.

New Year's Day in Africa

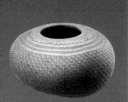

Gourd vessels like this one are displayed on Yoruba altars for special ceremonies. The Yorubaland New Year takes place in March, when villages and towns hold communal rites for the success of the next season's harvest.

Africa is a huge continent divided into many countries with different languages, religions, and traditions. This means that in Africa the New Year's holiday is celebrated in a variety of ways and at different times of the year. Many people join in the worldwide festivities on January 1. They celebrate with special food, dancing, drumming, and fireworks. These same people might also honor the traditional New Year's customs of their own communities, which are often linked with the beginning or end of farming seasons. Religious and spiritual ceremonies play a large part in many traditional New Year's celebrations.

Ethiopia

September marks Enkutatash, the Ethiopian Orthodox Christian New Year. It also celebrates new life, the blooming of the yellow daisies called maskal, and the end of the rainy season. On New Year's Eve, children offer songs and wishes for a long life to their neighbors. The children are given food or money in exchange. Then they go home for the New Year's ceremony of light. Each family member holds a torch made of sticks bound together. Some people whirl the torches to chase away the old year and welcome in the new. On New Year's Day, people bathe away last year's troubles in the river and put on new clothes. A family feast is prepared, which usually includes dorowot, a delicious spicy chicken dish. This is served with tella, a local beer. The meal is followed with coffee, which in Ethiopia takes a long time to prepare and serve. After the coffee ceremony, family elders bless the children.

DURING IBO NEW YEAR IN NIGERIA, children hide inside their homes as all sorts of odd sounds, such as doors banging and drums rolling, are heard in the street. They are explained as the grief of the old year as it leaves. When the sounds fade, everyone rushes outside to welcome the new year.

AFRICA

Africa lies south of Europe and west of Asia and contains 53 independent countries. Tropical rain forests dominate western and central Africa. The world's largest desert, the Sahara, stretches across northern Africa. Africa also has the world's longest river—the Nile. Much of the continent is grassland. In the north, most of the people are Arabs. The great majority of the African population lives south of the Sahara.

The yam is an important crop. The large tubers can be stored for two months. They also can be made into flour, which can last much longer. Yams may be broiled, boiled, fried, or roasted. This woman is using a mortar and pestle to pound boiled yams into flour.

This Ethiopian woman is performing the traditional coffee ceremony. A special place in the home is decorated with fresh long grass for this ritual, which may last up to two hours.

New Yams and New Year

The celebration of the yam harvest marks traditional New Year's festivities across much of West Africa. Some of the biggest festivities take place in Ghana, Nigeria, and Togo in August, September, or October.

The Muslim New Year

Millions of Africans are Muslims. They follow the teachings of Muhammad, the founder of Islam. Muslim New Year celebrates Muhammad's journey from Mecca to Medina in A.D. 622 (see pages 30–31). It is honored differently in each African Muslim community but always includes prayers at the mosque for the men. Many African Muslims also hold smaller, local New Year's celebrations at other times. These often mark the changing seasons. Mwaka Mpya is celebrated by Swahili of East Africa. Children often celebrate by running into the waters of the mangrove creeks along the coast.

The Djenne Mosque in Mali, West Africa, like other mosques, is central to Muslim celebration. Mosque architecture is different in each area, but all mosques are decorated with patterns rather than images of people. Many of the patterns celebrate God's gifts, such as fruits.

Cape Town Carnival

Cape Town's New Year's carnival is a dazzling parade of music, dance, and costume. It is held on January 1, as it has been since the late 1800's. The people who hold the carnival come from South Africa's mixed-race community. Long ago, they were slaves to white settlers. January 1 was the only holiday that the slaves were allowed. So they held a carnival to celebrate it, and to show the strength of their community. The carnival groups parade around their neighborhoods, singing and dancing. They receive festive food and drink in exchange.

Celebrating the Past—Looking to the Future

Among the Ewe people of Anlo in Ghana, New Year's is called Hogbetsotso. It begins on the first Saturday of November and honors a time when the people fled from a cruel ruler in the ancient Ewe city of Notsie, now in Togo. The women first softened the clay city walls with water. At midnight on the day of escape, Ewe leaders prayed by the soft city walls, then pierced them with daggers. The walls collapsed and the people fled. Hogbetsotso celebrations begin with sweeping all the Anlo villages. The dirt and dust, which represent all the bad things in life, are gathered into a pile and are said to be taken away by a special god. Then people honor the god Nyigbla, who helped to build the new Anlo city. The holiday is also marked by a celebration of peace and harmony. The rulers also tell their people about development projects for the year ahead.

People gather to listen to drumming and singing as the Anlo king arrives. The king represents the god Nyigbla. Women paint their bodies with fine patterns for the celebrations, far left. Necklaces show that the wearers are experienced in using the powers of spirits.

Each neighborhood in Cape Town, South Africa, has its own costume style and colors. Straw hats, parasols, and materials with patterns in primary colors are traditional carnival dress.

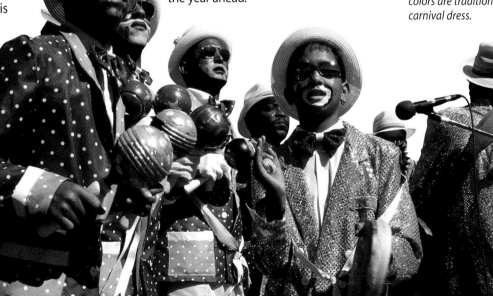

Australia and the Pacific

Many people in Australia and the Pacific Islands celebrate New Year's Day with a picnic on the beach.

Australasia and Oceania

With the exception of the vast Australian landmass—the world's largest island and smallest continent—the Pacific Ocean is sparsely dotted with thousands of small islands inhabited by peoples of diverse origin and traditions. In countries like Australia and New Zealand, which were colonized by European settlers, New Year's Day is celebrated on January 1, and many festivities are similar to those in Europe and North America. But among the native peoples, such as the Maoris of New Zealand, other New Year's holidays are celebrated in other ways. In recent years, immigrant communities have extended and enriched ideas about how and when the New Year's holiday can be celebrated.

AUSTRALASIA AND OCEANIA

Australasia and Oceania lie east of Asia and west of the Americas. Australasia refers to Australia, New Guinea, New Zealand, and other nearby islands. New Guinea and New Zealand are also considered as part of the Pacific Islands, or Oceania. Oceania is a name given to a group of many thousands of islands scattered across the Pacific Ocean. New Guinea is the largest island in the group. It contains Irian Jaya, which is a part of Indonesia, and the independent country of Papua New Guinea. Islands near the mainland of Asia (Indonesia, Japan, the Philippines) are part of Asia. Islands near North and South America (the Aleutians, the Galapagos) are grouped with those continents. Australia is itself a continent.

New Year's Day in the Southern Hemisphere

In Australia, New Zealand, and other countries in the South Pacific, New Year's Day falls during the hottest time of the year. Celebrations are held outside, and swimming and water skiing are high on many people's lists of New Year's Day activities. In Australia, New Year's Day may begin with a barbecue of grilled sausages, beef, chicken wings, and vegetables. Many families then head to the beach to spend the day in the coolest way possible.

This is a view of the beautiful fireworks display over Sydney Harbour, which every year marks the beginning of the new year in Australia.

A man prepares a typical barbeque breakfast outdoors. This is a popular way of spending New Year's Day morning for people in Australia, New Zealand, and other areas of the Pacific.

Fireworks over Sydney

In Australia, New Year's Eve celebrations are marked by a fantastic fireworks display over Sydney Harbour. Watching them is an annual ritual for many people. On New Year's Eve, the suburbs of Sydney are often deserted as people make their way to the city. Most watch the fireworks from near the Sydney Opera House. Many people actually camp there overnight to be sure of a good spot. The fireworks are fired from barges, bridges, and rooftops and are often accompanied by music at midnight. It is a spectacular sight!

Matariki

New Zealand lay uninhabited until about A.D. 1000, when a Polynesian people known as the Maoris arrived in their sturdy oceangoing canoes. When European settlers came in the 1800's, the Maori population declined rapidly, mainly because of European diseases, such as tuberculosis, to which the local peoples had no immunity. For a while it seemed that the Maori people would become extinct. But during the 1900's, the population began to grow again. In the final decades of the 1900's, the Maori also began to reassert the uniqueness of their culture and sought to preserve or revive as much of it as possible. The wider celebration of Matariki, or Maori New Year, is one result of this.

How the Festival Is Celebrated

Matariki is the Maori name for the Pleiades or Seven Sisters, a cluster of stars in the Taurus constellation. New Year's Day is celebrated on the first new moon after these stars appear in the eastern horizon just before dawn. This happens shortly before the winter solstice in June. Traditionally, the festival was marked with sorrow for those who had died since the last new year, and by singing, dancing, and feasting to mark the passing of winter.

The traditional Maori greeting is called a hongi and involves two people pressing their noses together. It is a symbol of welcome and friendship.

MATARIKI IS WIDELY CELEBRATED IN THE PACIFIC, where it is also known as Matali'I, Mataliki, Makali'I, and Makahiki.

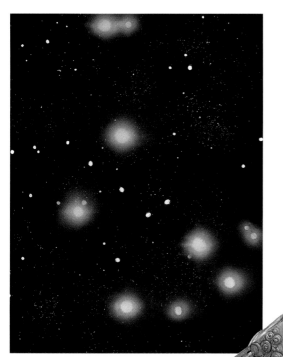

The Pleiades is a cluster of stars in the constellation of Taurus the Bull. The appearance of these stars on the eastern horizon signifies the beginning of the Maori New Year.

Papuan Celebrations

The Gogodala people of the Gulf of Papua in Papua New Guinea have some of the world's most remarkably carved canoes. Canoe prows often represent the open-jawed mouth of a crocodile or lizard eating a long-necked human head. These canoes are used in ceremonial races. Since the 1970's, they have come to mark celebrations such as New Year's Day and Christmas.

A decorative prow adorns a Gogodala canoe used in canoe races to celebrate the new year in the Papuan Gulf.

The Maori meeting-house forms an important part of traditional Maori life. These houses, believed to be sacred places, are usually elaborately carved both inside and outside. New Year's celebrations are often held in these houses.

Glossary

Altar A table or raised platform on which offerings are placed, usually found in churches or temples.

Ancestor A family member from a preceding generation to whom you are directly related, for example, a grandfather or great-grandfather.

Astrological ritual A set of actions done in a precise way to predict future events by looking at the position of the stars, which are believed to influence human life.

Atonement The restoration of peace and harmony or favorable relations with God.

Auspicious Bringing good luck.

Blessing Divine favor or protection.

Ceremony The celebration of an important event with an act or series of acts that follow a set of instructions established by a religion, culture, or country.

Chastisement Punishment.

Colonize To establish a settlement in a new country and to impose the newcomers' government or culture on the native people of that country.

Constellation A group of stars with fixed positions that form an imaginary shape in the sky.

Devotee A person who practices his or her religion with strong belief and performs ceremonies and rituals closely following all of that religion's laws and customs.

Dialect A local or regional variation of a language.

Elder An older person who is respected for his or her experience and wisdom.

Equinox Either of the two days of the year when the sun is directly above Earth's equator. On these days, the day and night are of nearly equal length everywhere on Earth. The equinoxes occur on March 19, 20, or 21 and on September 22 or 23.

Farming cycle The period from one planting time to the next in which a series of activities like plowing the land and harvesting are carried out.

Fast To choose to go without eating for a time for religious reasons.

Fate A power beyond human control believed by some to determine the events in a person's life.

Fertility The ability to produce and reproduce things. Land is fertile when many crops can grow there.

Fortune Happiness or good luck that happens in a person's life.

Fortune-telling Telling or claiming to tell what will happen in the future.

Icon An image of a god or deity that is considered sacred and is given special respect.

Immortal Living forever, something that never dies.

Immunity The condition of being free of punishment or the harmful effects of sickness or disease.

Incense A material made from gum or wood that produces perfumed smoke when it is burned.

Indigenous people Natives, the original people living in a country or area before other people settled there, and their descendants.

Leap year A year that has an extra period of time than an ordinary year. In the Gregorian calendar (which normally has 365 days), a leap year occurs every 4 years and has 366 days. The extra day has been added to make up for the extra quarter of a day in the solar calendar.

Longevity Long life.

Lunar calendar A calendar that marks the passing of years by following the phases of the moon. Lunar calendars are still used today by some religions and cultures.

Martyr A person who willingly accepts punishment or death rather than reject his or her religious beliefs.

Migrate To move to a new area or country in search of work or better living conditions.

Missionary A person sent by a religious group to preach a faith and to convert others to that faith.

Monastery A place where a community of religious people (usually monks) live.

Mourning A period following a person's death during which people express deep sorrow and perform special rituals in observance of that death.

Omen A message or event believed to be a sign of what will happen in the future.

Orbit The path of Earth or another heavenly body as it circles around the sun or another body.

Pagan A person who is not, for example, a Christian, Jew, or Muslim and who may worship many gods or no god. Modern pagans practice some forms of ancient religions.

Patriarch A father or male ruler of a family or community.

Penitential With deep regret or sorrow for sins committed.

Procession A parade held for a religious ceremony or ritual.

Prophet A person who has been inspired by God and communicates God's will or interprets God's message to the people.

Prosperity The condition of having good luck and success.

Prow The front part of a ship or boat.

Redemption Forgiveness of sins or the freedom from punishment.

Reforestation Planting or seeding trees to grow again in an area where they once grew.

Refugee A person who has left his or her community or country to escape danger.

Repentance Being sorry for doing wrong.

Revelation The act of communicating a divine truth.

Ritual A set of repeated actions done in a precise way with a special religious meaning or significance.

Salutation Greeting.

Shaman A priest or medicine man who uses magic to protect people and to cure the sick.

Solar calendar A calendar that marks the passing of years by measuring the time it takes Earth to revolve completely around the sun, about 365 and one-fourth days. The Julian calendar, established by Julius Caesar in 46 B.C., and the Gregorian calendar, established by Pope Gregory XIII in 1582, are two examples.

Solstice A time of year at the halfway mark between the two equinoxes, when the sun is at its northernmost or southernmost position. There are two solstices in a year. In the Northern Hemisphere the summer solstice is on June 20, 21, or 22, and the winter solstice is on December 21 or 22.

Superstition A belief or practice that is the result of an unreasonable fear. The belief that magic affects events.

Index